TEETH

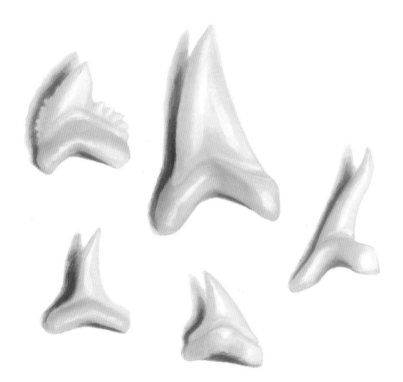

Sneed B. Collard III

TEETH

Illustrated by Phyllis V. Saroff

Charlesbridge

For Joan Stevenson, who knows how to
sink her teeth into a good book!

     —Love, Sneed

For my mother.

     —P. V. S.

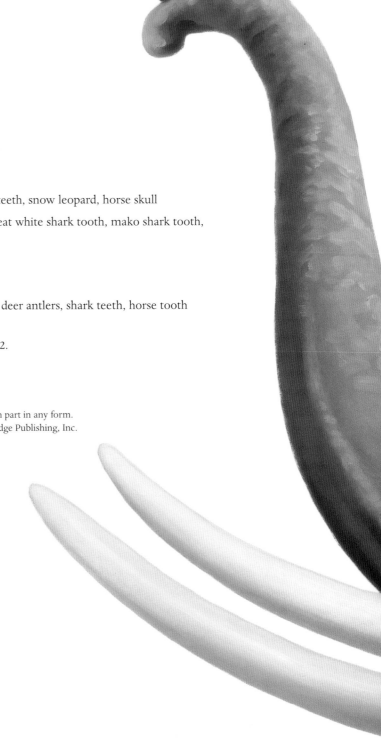

Cover illustrations: five-lined skink with cricket, shark teeth, snow leopard, horse skull

Half title page illustrations (clockwise from center): great white shark tooth, mako shark tooth, bull shark tooth, lemon shark tooth, tiger shark tooth

Full title page: Cuban crocodile

Pages 4–5: African elephant

Page 31 (from top): ram horn, horse skull, white-tailed deer antlers, shark teeth, horse tooth

Boldface words can be found in the glossary on page 32.

Text copyright © 2008 by Sneed B. Collard III
Illustrations copyright © 2008 by Phyllis V. Saroff
All rights reserved, including the right of reproduction in whole or in part in any form.
Charlesbridge and colophon are registered trademarks of Charlesbridge Publishing, Inc.

Published by Charlesbridge
85 Main Street
Watertown, MA 02472
(617) 926-0329
www.charlesbridge.com

Library of Congress Cataloging-in-Publication Data
Collard, Sneed B.
 Teeth / Sneed B. Collard III ; illustrated by Phyllis Saroff.
  p. cm.
 ISBN: 978-1-58089-120-2 (reinforced for library use)
 ISBN: 978-1-58089-121-9 (softcover)
1. Teeth—Juvenile literature. I. Saroff, Phyllis V., ill. II. Title.
QL858.C55 2008
591.4'4—dc22   2007002266

Printed in China
(hc) 10 9 8 7 6 5 4 3 2 1
(sc) 10 9 8 7 6 5 4 3 2 1

Illustrations done in Alkyds on Arches hot-press watercolor paper
Display type and text type set in Dante MT
Color separations by Chroma Graphics, Singapore
Printed and bound by Jade Productions
Production supervision by Brian G. Walker
Designed by Martha MacLeod Sikkema

It's hard to imagine life without teeth. Look around. Many animals have them. That's no surprise, because teeth do many amazing things.

Teeth slice.

Vampire Bats

Vampires are bats that drink blood.
A vampire bat lands next to a sleeping
deer or cow and crawls up to it. With its
razor-sharp front **teeth**, or **incisors**, the bat
slices through the animal's skin and then laps up
the blood that flows out. However, vampire bats rarely drink enough blood
to harm their victims. And don't worry—these bats almost never attack people.

Teeth stab.

Snow Leopard

The upper **canines**, or eyeteeth, of snow leopards and other wild cats are longer than the canines of most other mammals. They have to be! A snow leopard often hunts ibex, a type of wild goat, and wild sheep that are up to three times its size. The cat's long canines help it stab, hang on to, and kill these formidable animals. Canines also help the leopard snag marmots, hares, and other small prey.

Teeth crack.

Spotted Hyena

Many animals can bite, but hyenas can BITE! They have powerful jaws, and their back teeth, called **molars** and **premolars**, have exceptionally hard tops, or crowns. Hyenas use these teeth not only to eat meat but also to crack and crush up the bones of zebras and other large hoofed animals. With teeth this strong, hyenas rarely leave leftovers.

And they grind, mash, and munch.

Domestic Horse

Grasses contain **silica** (SIH-lih-kuh)—the same substance found in sand. Silica makes grasses difficult to grind up, but horse teeth are up to the task. Horse teeth are topped with interweaving ridges of **enamel** that form rough surfaces for grinding and mashing food. Unlike human jaws, horse jaws move from side to side as they chew. This gives them extra grinding power.

Teeth can be very different.

Human

A single mammal can have several different kinds of teeth. Humans are a good example. We each have incisors for cutting food. We have canines for stabbing and tearing. We also have premolars and molars for chewing, crushing, and grinding. Having these different kinds of teeth allows us—and many other mammals— to dine on a huge variety of chow, from fruits and vegetables to grains and meat.

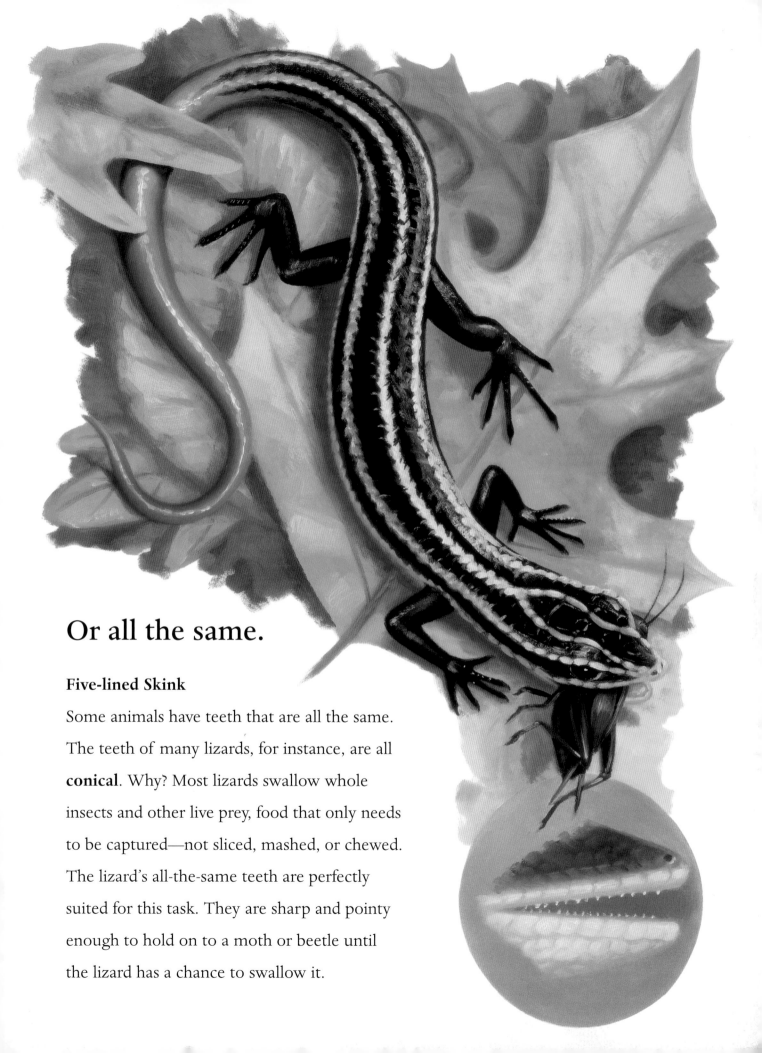

Or all the same.

Five-lined Skink

Some animals have teeth that are all the same.
The teeth of many lizards, for instance, are all
conical. Why? Most lizards swallow whole
insects and other live prey, food that only needs
to be captured—not sliced, mashed, or chewed.
The lizard's all-the-same teeth are perfectly
suited for this task. They are sharp and pointy
enough to hold on to a moth or beetle until
the lizard has a chance to swallow it.

Teeth can be small.

Bullfrog

With a lightning-fast lunge or flick of the tongue, a frog pulls
an insect into its mouth. Like lizards, frogs don't need teeth
for stabbing, chewing, or slicing. In fact, some don't need
teeth at all. Over millions of years many frogs and toads
have lost their teeth altogether. Others have teeth only
on their upper jaws. When frogs and toads do have teeth,
they are very small—just big enough to hang on to insects
and other lively prey before gulping them down.

And very large.

Asian Elephant

Elephants eat coarse plant materials such as grass, twigs, and bark. These large mammals come equipped with six pairs of molars in each jaw but use only the front pair for grinding and mashing food. When this pair wears down, it falls out and the teeth behind it move forward. The last molars are the biggest. Each one can weigh up to nine pounds. After the last molars are worn away, the elephant weakens from hunger and dies. By the way, if you're wondering about an elephant's **tusks**, keep reading. . . .

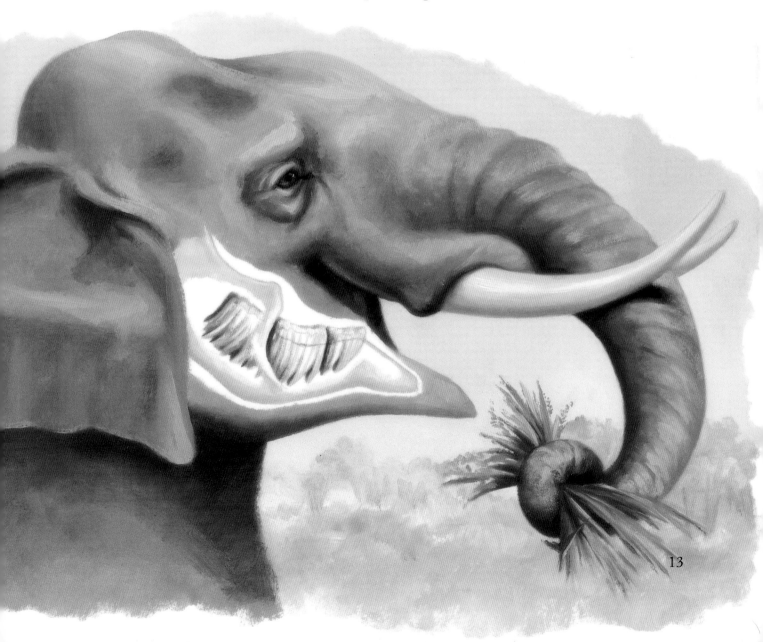

Tusks are teeth.

Atlantic Walrus

A walrus's tusks can grow up to three feet long. Elephant tusks are even longer. One African elephant grew tusks that stretched over eleven feet long and weighed more than two hundred pounds! An elephant's tusks are long incisors, but a walrus's tusks are upper canines. A walrus uses its tusks to haul itself onto ice floes or up onto the beach. During mating season a male flashes his tusks to drive other males away from the females with which he wants to mate. Tusks are formidable weapons, and male walruses often hurt or kill each other during fights over mates.

So are fangs.

Western Diamondback Rattlesnake

Like a leopard's canines, a snake's **fangs** stab. Snakes use their fangs to defend themselves against hungry birds and other predators. Fangs also allow snakes to grasp and kill their own prey. Venomous snakes have especially interesting fangs. Their fangs are hollow and act as hypodermic needles, injecting venom into enemies or prey such as rodents and birds.

Antlers and horns are not teeth—but you probably knew that already.

Moose

Do you know the difference between **antlers**, **horns**, and teeth? Teeth—such as a walrus's tusks or a snake's fangs—grow out of an animal's mouth. They usually have a core made of **pulp** and outer coverings made of hard **dentin** and enamel. Antlers and horns, though, grow out of an animal's skull, and most are made of bone and a hard substance called **keratin**. Moose and most other members of the deer family have antlers. Bighorn sheep and goats have horns. What's the difference between antlers and horns? Antlers are shed each year. Horns are not.

17

Two teeth. . . .

Narwhale

A narwhale doesn't need teeth to hunt the squid and fish it eats, but it has two upper front teeth just the same. One of these teeth stays small and isn't used for anything. But in male narwhales the other tooth grows into a grooved "spear" measuring more than eight feet in length. No one is sure what purpose this strange tooth serves, but it probably helps male narwhales attract mates and fend off competing males.

Twenty teeth. . . .

Aye-aye

Aye-ayes (EYE-eyes) come equipped with either
eighteen or twenty teeth. These strange tree-dwelling
animals live only in Madagascar and, unlike any other
primates, have claws on the ends of their long, slender
fingers. The claws help the aye-aye probe holes in tree trunks
for insects and insect larvae. What if an aye-aye can't reach an insect?
No problem. The aye-aye uses its powerful front incisors to tear away
the bark of the tree and grabs the meal hidden beneath it.

Forty-eight teeth. . . .

Orca

Forty-four is the standard number of teeth our mammal ancestors had. These included twelve incisors, four canines, sixteen premolars, and twelve molars. Through millions of years of evolution, many mammals—including narwhales, aye-ayes, and humans—have permanently lost some or all of these teeth. However, most orcas have gained teeth. A typical orca has between forty and fifty-six teeth, with forty-eight being the most common number.

A whole lot of teeth!

Great White Shark

Some sharks have so many teeth it's a wonder that they all fit into their mouths! A great white shark can have as many as three thousand teeth arranged in several rows. A shark's front row of teeth is used to capture sea lions and other prey. The shark also uses its teeth to tear apart its food and defend itself from enemies. New teeth constantly grow behind the older ones. When a shark loses a tooth, a new one moves up and forward to replace it.

21

Over time, teeth wear away.

Tuatara

Tuataras may look like lizards, but they belong to their own order of reptiles. They live only in New Zealand, where they feed on insects, eggs, and baby birds. A tuatara has three rows of teeth—two in its upper jaw and one in its lower jaw. However, a tuatara only gets one set of teeth in its lifetime. Since tuataras can live for many decades, their single set of teeth can become extremely worn as they get older.

Some get replaced.

Cuban Crocodile

Unlike tuatara teeth, the teeth of crocodiles and most other reptiles get replaced. Crocodile teeth are solid but have hollow roots. New teeth are formed in special folds of the mouth located below the old teeth and eventually fill the hollow roots. At regular intervals, when an old tooth falls out, a new one pushes up to replace it. Crocodiles don't lose all their teeth at once. Usually only every other tooth is lost at the same time. That way crocodiles always have at least half of their teeth to hunt.

Others keep growing and growing.

Hippopotamus

Hippopotamuses spend a huge part of their lives eating. That's no surprise when you look at their size! Like any other teeth, hippo teeth constantly wear down from use. Fortunately hippos have a set of incisors and canines that are constantly growing. This ensures that a hippo will never run out of teeth. The teeth of horses and many other grazing animals also keep growing throughout the animals' lives.

Some tongues have teeth.

Cutthroat Trout

We're used to thinking about teeth growing only from jaws, but that's not always true. Some fish have teeth that grow from their tongues! Fish use these "tongue teeth" to hold on to prey. But those aren't the only places fish teeth grow. . . .

So do some throats.

Bullnose Ray

Like sharks, rays and skates are fish. Most search along
the sea bottom for clams and other hard-shelled animals.
Cracking this food open might be a problem, but
rays and skates have hard flat teeth in their throats.
These flat "crushers" crack even the hardest
shells and allow skates and rays to devour
the soft-bodied animals inside.

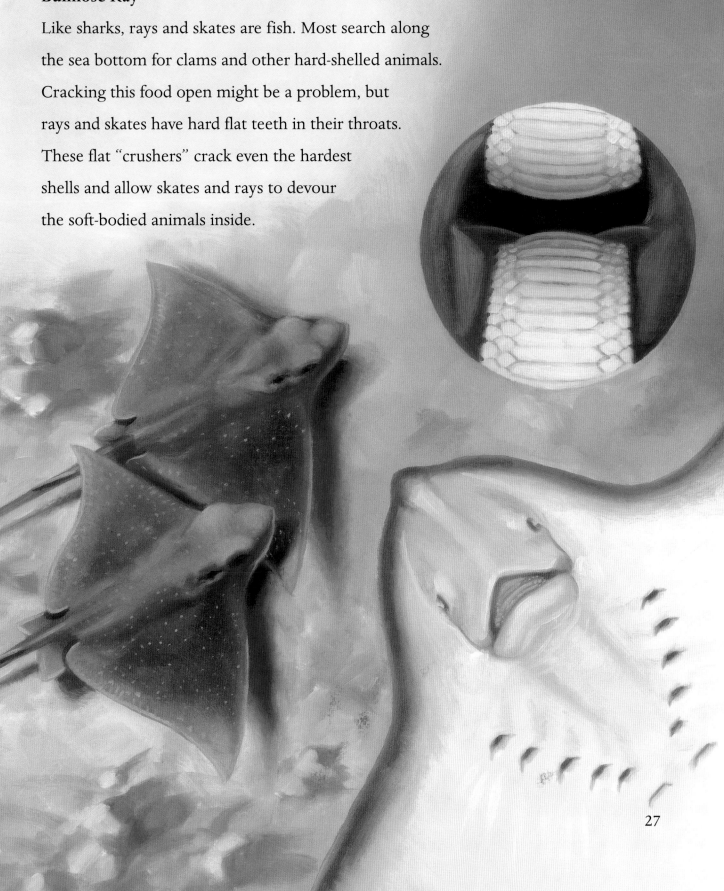

Of course, teeth can do lots more. Teeth can be angry.

Alaskan Brown Bear

Teeth can be formidable weapons. Most animals try to avoid fighting as much as possible, but they sometimes have to threaten or warn other animals to stay away. Teeth come in handy for this. When a bear shows a mouthful of sharp teeth, it sends a clear message: "Stay away if you don't want trouble."

Or glad.

Chimpanzee

Just as teeth can spell danger, they can also show friendliness.
Chimpanzees and many other primates live in close social
groups. In these groups it's important for everyone to get
along. If a chimp smiles at other chimps, it shows that he's
friendly and means no harm.

And when they fall out, teeth can be *very* lucky.

People are among many kinds of mammals that get two complete sets of teeth. A set of twenty baby teeth lasts for several years and then falls out, one tooth at a time. A set of thirty-two permanent adult teeth replaces the baby teeth. People have invented fun traditions about the loss of baby teeth. In many countries a child places a baby tooth under her pillow. During the night the tooth fairy, or in some countries the tooth mouse or the tooth bird, takes the tooth and, with luck, leaves money in its place!

Teeth.
Don't you wish you
had more?

Resources

Beeler, Selby B. *Throw Your Tooth on the Roof: Tooth Traditions from Around the World*. Boston: Houghton Mifflin, 1998.

Dental Anatomy
http://www.vivo.colostate.edu/hbooks/pathphys/digestion/pregastric/dentalanat.html
Learn about the anatomy of human and animal teeth.

KidsHealth: The Truth About Teeth
http://www.kidshealth.org/kid/body/teeth_noSW.html
Find out how teeth aid in talking and how to take care of your teeth.

Lynch, Wayne. *Whose Teeth are These?* Milwaukee, WI: Gareth Stevens, 2003.

Showers, Paul. *How Many Teeth?* (Let's-Read-and-Find-Out Science Book). New York: HarperCollins, 1991.

Swanson, Diane. *Teeth That Stab and Grind* (Up Close series). Vancouver, Canada: Greystone Books, 2000.

University of Adelaide:
Animal Dentition Sources
http://www.adelaide.edu.au/library/guide/med/dent/animaldent.html
Choose from these links to find different sources for various animal dentition sites.

University of Michigan Museum of Zoology's Animal Diversity Web: Introduction to Teeth
http://animaldiversity.ummz.umich.edu/site/topics/mammal_anatomy/tooth_introduction.html
Learn about the different types of teeth that mammals have.

Glossary

antlers: Bony projections that grow out of the skulls of some animals. Antlers are shed every year.

canines: Cone-shaped, usually large teeth located near the front of the mouth. Canines are used for stabbing prey and tearing apart meat.

conical: Cone-shaped.

dentin: The bonelike material that forms the main structure of a tooth and is located beneath the enamel.

enamel: The smooth and extremely hard outer layer of a tooth above the gum line. Enamel protects the tooth from wear and decay.

fangs: Long sharp teeth used for stabbing and, in some cases, injecting venom into prey.

horns: Bony projections that grow from an animal's skull. Unlike antlers, horns are not shed.

incisors: Front teeth used mostly for cutting.

keratin: A strong protein that helps form antlers, horns, hair, and nails.

molars: Back teeth used for grinding and chewing.

premolars: Teeth used for grinding and chewing that are located in front of the molars.

pulp: The central part of a tooth, containing nerves and blood vessels. Pulp is made of soft tissue that supplies essential blood and other nutrients to the cells of the tooth.

silica: A crystalline compound that's found in sand, quartz, and grass.

teeth: Hard, bonelike structures located in an animal's mouth or throat. Teeth aid in biting and chewing food and are also used to catch prey, to defend against enemies, and to send messages to other animals.

tusks: Large teeth that stick out from an animal's mouth even when the mouth is closed. Tusks can be used to obtain food, show off to mates, drive away competitors, and defend against attackers.